The Golf Letters
Tee Tales

The Golf Letters
Tee Tales

Annie Loughlin
LPGA/PGA

LOUGHLIN GOLF PRESS 2010

First Edition

ISBN
978-1-4507-3401-1

Printed in the USA by Fidlar Printing Company, Davenport, IA

www.loughlingolf.com

❦❧

Table of Contents

❃❧❧❃

Foreword

by Steven Pressfield

I'VE TAKEN LESSONS from a lot of pros over the years. Ann Loughlin is the best I've ever worked with, and when you read this book you'll understand why.

Golf is a game of imperfection. Imperfection equals humor. *The Golf Letters* is loaded with that commodity and what's best is it's "Annie's humor." Ms. A. Loughlin, LPGA/PGA, sees the world through her own quirky prism. Not every vignette in this collection is a belly laugh or a knee-slapper; many are wry observations, subtle commentary. The humor arises out of innocent misunderstandings, sudden insights and the curious ways that golf humbles and enlightens us all. The story of the baby owl is like a Zen koan; there's more wisdom in its few short paragraphs than in entire novels. Annie's "comma story" (I'll say no more) is worth the price of admission all by itself.

What makes Annie so good on the lesson tee is not just her knowledge of the swing and the game, though these are deep and abundant, but her capacity to put the student at ease. Golf is scary. A session on the practice range can reduce captains of industry to jibbering wrecks. Annie presides over this precinct without judgment. Her calm, easy-going presence makes that self-imposed pressure go away. We can listen. We can hear her. (Who else but Annie would put a marshmallow on a tee to get a student to lighten up?) And she listens to us.

I've taken lessons from pros who knew their stuff inside and out, who were superb players and practitioners—but they couldn't put what they knew into words. They couldn't reach the student. If you study with Annie, you learn right away that one of her mantras is, "Keep your grip pressure light." She has a drill where you take your grip and hold the club vertically in front of you, using only as much pressure as it takes to keep the stick balanced. Got it? That's the pressure Annie wants you to use in a full swing, no more.

Why is this important? Because the hands, as Bagger Vance once said, are our connection to the world outside ourselves. They're the yoke where the golfer and the club come together. (Myself, I'm a born white-knuckler; I snatch that club in a death grip. No wonder my backswing takes 0.3 seconds.) Annie understands—and makes us understand—that the lighter the pressure, the less tension in the forearms, shoulders and back and the more powerful the swing. But there's more to this than golf or competitiveness or the pursuit of excellence. It's Annie's way of looking at life—a keep-it-simple, less-is-more, the-game-is-supposed-to-be-fun approach that concentrates our focus onto the one simple action that lets a hundred others fall into place all by themselves.

Many of the stories in *The Golf Letters* are about kids. I can't imagine a better guide for a pint-sized linkster than Annie, because Annie is a kid herself. She loves the guileless turns of phrase that pop out of children's mouths. And because she's such a great listener, she can tune in to the amazing inner worlds that kids bring, in all their innocence, to the golf course and to life.

The Golf Letters isn't instruction. It's not "tips" or fixes or how-to's. But you may find, as I did, when you've finished reading it, that you learned more about golf—and life—than you did from a summer of lessons or a library full of books. Enjoy!

Steven Pressfield
Author of *The Legend of Bagger Vance, The War of Art* and many best-selling historical novels

Introduction

MY PASSIONS ARE golf, life and stories. How fortunate then, for me to present *The Golf Letters,* which embrace and entwine these three passions. Teaching golf has been my career for 22 years. Golf's aura, soul, charisma, charm, simplicity, complication, subtleties, intricacies, and elusiveness are the characteristics I've tried to portray in *The Golf Letters*.

After observing thousands of hooks, slices, topped balls, fat shots, pushes, fades, missed putts, made putts, cries of anguish, cries of delight, frustrations, joys, thrills and so much more, I realize that the complex nature of the game can better be understood through the storied description of all these facets.

Golf goes beyond sport. It goes beyond the physical and mental challenges provided. Golf pierces the very heart of a person's being. Handling adversity and challenge through the game of golf helps mold and define a person's character.

I am an educator of golf. I am a woman who teaches people to get a grip! I have observed young and old, male and female, athletic and non-athletic, intelligent and average, strong and weak, and business-oriented and blue-collar all rise to meet golf's challenge.

Golf provides a chance to find that perfect shot, make that perfect swing, and hole that perfect putt. It provides a moment where pure bliss might be encountered. The striving in golf becomes worthwhile when this happens.

Daily endeavors oftentimes do not provide these opportunities.

Golf began in Scotland in the 12th century and its tradition is honored. The conquest of nature and one's own mind become paramount. This is the age-old quest played out on fairways and greens around the world.

Through the years, many students have not understood me when I explained they would never conquer golf. I explained that golf would always be the winner. Along the way, though, if the student could allow and accept what the game presented, *they* would be victorious, regardless of score. It's the little things in golf that matter. Gaining respect for these nuances and subtleties has been a part of the task of teaching this game.

With all of this laid out before me, I embarked on my career. I've gained extreme satisfaction in guiding students through all the physical and psychological obstacles.

The satisfaction for me is when a student returns and describes the round they played incorporating what they learned in the lesson. Some even tell how they shot the best score of their life because of my help. The joys come in taking a new student and introducing a sport that will encompass a lifetime of thrills, camaraderie and challenge.

I work with people's fears and see how they accomplish what they thought was impossible.

These are treasured moments. Some are life changing. To be a part of that has been a gift, indeed.

Teaching golf has enriched my life. I hope it has enriched the lives of the many I have crossed paths with. I would like to say thank you and tell you a bit about how I arrived at this place.

Independent teaching professionals are almost extinct now. We're almost like the dinosaur. But we have stories. Oh, do we have stories. Being an elder stateswoman in my field, I feel worthy to share some of these stories with you. I want to tell you just a bit about the path I have taken.

I always loved golf. However, I went to college pre-Title IX and there were no opportunities for women in sport in the early 1970s. My uncles were all top amateur golfers in Iowa. In college, they captained the Notre Dame and Georgetown golf teams. One competed against Jack Nicklaus and lost by a stroke in the national amateur tournament.

I went to college, obtained my Masters degree and worked in education at the college level before becoming a golf professional. I loved teaching and wanted to find that career in golf. Luckily, I was able to mentor under Barbra O'Brien in San Jose, California, and build a teaching business. My career has allowed me to caddy on the LPGA tour, play in pro ams across the country, and teach golf schools in Arizona, California, Montana, Connecticut, Iowa and Minnesota. I have coordinated golf travel to Idaho, Arizona, California, and Ireland. Ah, yes, Ireland. I've probably played 25 of the links courses in Ireland. They remain my absolute favorites. I would say traveling to Ireland to play golf remains the highlight of my golf career.

I've been blessed with meeting lots of interesting people and attending lots of fun cocktail parties. And in between there were the tournaments, the seminars, the clinics, the trips, the teaching and the consoling and celebrating with students.

I've played golf with Billy Collins, national poet laureate, author Steven Pressfield, Hollywood agent and producer Nancy Roberts, golfer Kathy Whitworth, singer Jerry Jeff Walker, baseball player Rick Sutcliffe, U.S. Open winner Steve Jones, and Shirley Spork, one of LPGA's founders, to name a few.

I've watched Arnold Palmer, Annika Sorenstam, Lorena Ochoa, Tiger Woods, Sam Snead, Byron Nelson, and many other professionals play golf. I've socialized with former USGA president Judy Bell and have the autographs of Nancy Lopez, Patty Sheehan and Geoff Ogilvy. I've sat and had a beer with Senator Christopher Dodd in Ireland.

I've watched Olympic champions Pablo Morales and Kristi Yamaguchi hit balls. I've caddied in Boca Raton, Florida when the Challenger fell to the sea and saw the immediate aftermath. I've run into rock star Huey Lewis, actor Jim Nabors, golfer Notah Begay, tennis analyst Cliff Drysdale, Olympic swimmer Mark Spitz, and the Dalai Lama. I've caddied in the LPGA group Hall of Famer Sandra Palmer played in. I've played in a pro am with Tommy Smothers.

Beyond all of this is the chance I've had to teach so many who have a passion to both learn and play the game. This has been the real thrill.

I became the fifth woman in California to obtain PGA Class A status in 1989. Becoming an elder stateswoman in golf has taken time. I have endured, observed, and compiled. I look back over this landscape and remember the personalities, the venues, the tales of woe and glee, the golfers' laments and joys, and I see a pattern. It is a pattern of human tendencies played out in the game of golf.

I've listened closely to countless students' hopes and dreams, and always done everything I could to help them come true. I've offered a lot of advice. I've offered a lot of encouragement. It has been loads of fun.

The following musings, vignettes, comments and stories will provide you with a glimpse of this life of mine. So, please sit back and enjoy these musings of mine, as I surely have!

❧❧❧

The Eagle

THE EAGLE. THERE it was, circling overhead as I played an early morning round of golf this past August. I noticed the eagle at the start of the round, off in the distance, flying out over the river. The round went on and by the eighth hole, I was into a wonderful rythym successfully incorporating an epiphany into my swing. The world was rosy!

Suddenly, as I prepared to hit my second shot on the par four eighth hole, I looked up and the eagle was circling directly overhead. It then flew to a nearby telephone pole and perched. I addressed my ball and with my newfound pure swing, hit a shot that sailed directly at the flagstick and yes…disappeared.

I held my breath as I zoomed up to the green and walked to the hole, not daring to hope it had gone in. It had. I had my eagle. I took the ball out of the hole. As I turned to high-five my companions, I saw the grand eagle still watching from its perch atop the telephone pole. Eagles, eagles everywhere!

It is for these elusive and unscripted moments that I play and teach golf. They can appear anywhere at anytime and our job is to be ready and attentive, and nothing more. Golf is the perfect chance to practice this art, and if we keep on, we will reap the rewards!

❧❧❧❧

Remember, You're Not Chi Chi

NOT EVERYTHING YOU read in the golf magazines is going to make you a better golfer. One story that really gets the point across is the following.

I was giving lessons to a woman who was always trying to improve, just like all of us.

One day, she was sitting in a dental office and picked up a golf magazine. In it, she found an article about Chi Chi Rodriguez driving the ball. He mentioned that using very, very long tees would result in more distance.

This woman thought she would do the same, and went out and bought some very, very long tees. She used them in her lesson and again in her league play. She really hoped to improve. She struggled with her driver and was willing to try anything. She figured if the extra long tees worked for Chi Chi they surely would work for her.

She told me that she teed up the ball on the first tee of league and took a swing. The tee flew about halfway down the fairway, while the ball plopped down directly below where she teed it up. It was like the old magic trick where the magician pulls the tablecloth out from under the china dishes and the dishes remain intact.

So, the whole thing backfired for her. The darn tee was so long that her club went completely underneath it. It probably worked for Chi Chi because he is a professional and he hits the ball on the upswing. He wanted the ball higher at address. This was his personal preference.

However, when golfers read golf magazines, they must be sure to realize that the drills and information are not for everybody. It might even be a good idea to double check with your teaching professional before you incorporate any of the suggestions in these articles.

So, tee it high and let it fly, but, remember to use golf "tips" judiciously.

❧❦❧❦

All the Way to China

THE FUNNY STORIES about golfers are endless. Some of the things I have observed and encountered on the lesson tee have given me pause.

I have had many a chance to observe my share of golf lessons through the years, and to say that golfers say the darndest things would be an understatement to wit:

A golf student who barely played much was struggling with making solid contact with the ball. She continued hitting behind the ball and digging up huge divots.

After one final and hefty swing, another big chunk of dirt and earth flew out from behind the ball. The woman bent over, gazed into the ground where she had dug the huge divots and holes, looked up at me and said calmly, "I think I see Chinese people!"

❦❦❦❦

Lessons for a 5-Year-Old

WE ALL LOVE golf. And, some parents love golf so much that they want their sons and daughters to take up the game. This is all well and good.

However, we might examine how some parents go about exposing their children to the game of golf.

The main thing about being a child, which by the way, only occurs once in a person's lifetime, is that the child gets to experience life as fun. If the child does not have this experience as a child, it becomes that much more difficult to experience any form of fun as an adult.

The parents' job is to provide boundaries and guidelines for the child, but in learning a new sport, it is imperative that the child experience the joy of the sport. The technicalities of the sport should come in second place at this point. Otherwise, they miss the real essence and fun of the game.

A cautionary tale follows.

A father in California wanted his daughter to learn golf. He called me on the telephone and began the conversation this way:

"I want my daughter to have lessons from an LPGA professional now, because I have taken her as far as I can take her with instruction."

I responded, "Ok, I will get my lesson book and we can schedule her to begin lessons."

I asked the father when would be a good day and time to begin.

The father replied, "Well, she gets out of kindergarten every day at noon."

Oh my. I was aghast. Here was a 5-year old child being signed up for technical golf lessons by her father as he had hopes of million dollar paychecks for the girl. All the wrong reasons for taking golf lessons.

By then it was too late for me to say no, so I scheduled the lesson. The father and daughter came to the lesson. The father stood by as the little girl took the lesson. He sternly told her to "pay attention now" as I tried to encourage fun during the lesson. The father would have none of it, as he wanted a serious lesson where no fun was involved. The little girl smiled and laughed, as she exclaimed in delight, "Oh, look at the pretty butterfly."

The father once again admonished her, "Now, pay attention."

I did what I could to encourage fun while still learning, but I had the father and his expectations to deal with.

One time, around 9:00 pm on a school night, I observed the father and his daughter at the driving range, getting a basket of golf balls so she could practice. The little 5-year old was barely big enough to hold the basket and she looked very unhappy and tired.

More than likely she did not continue with her golf. If she did, she probably found no joy in golf. Her father had become a stern taskmaster. He pursued the understanding of golf mechanics at the cost of enjoyment of the game.

This is a cautionary tale. A parent needs to be sure when they involve their children in golf that they encourage fun. This makes the game a lifetime sport. What follows will follow, be it a college scholarship, the LPGA or PGA tour, club membership golf, public course golf, golf with friends, or golf occasionally.

P.S. I want to add a footnote. Every 5-year old I teach private lessons to points out a pretty butterfly nearby. Isn't this interesting?

❧❦❦❧

Silver Dollars

HERE'S THE STORY of a California golfer who decided to sign on for some golf lessons with me. He had observed me giving lessons daily when he came to the range to hit lots of buckets of balls. I mean, this guy hit lots of golf balls. Probably hundreds per day and it took him all afternoon or evening.

The fellow would spend hours on the range working on various aspects of his golf swing. He also appeared to be self-taught. Occasionally, I would glance over at him and he would be intently examining one of the many positions of the golf club in the full swing.

So, the lessons began. I worked for about a month or so on various parts of the golf swing with him and I attempted, in addition, to get him to let go of his various fixations about certain swing positions. He was getting mentally stuck.

We would work on swing speed and he would go home with a couple of drills to work on, but before he left the lesson, he would say, "Ok, but what about my follow through?" "What about the backswing?" "What about my grip?"

After working through all of the swing for over a month or maybe more, I suggested that the golfer take his swing to the golf course and see how it held up there.

The golfer looked at me and said, "Oh, I don't PLAY golf, I just work on my golf swing here on the driving range!"

This was a shocker for me. After all, what was the point, I thought.

With that in mind, he continued to take lessons, but I was getting tired of going over and over all the same mechanics, and felt there was no point. After all, he didn't even play golf.

However, I persevered, because I realized each golfer has his own set of goals. As long as he was happy, I would keep working with him.

One day, he came to the lesson, and said, "Here, this is for you." He handed me a box and inside were three silver dollars over a hundred years old encased in preservative plastic.

"These are for you since you helped me so much with my golf swing," he replied. "Now I am done with the lessons and thank you very much."

The lesson here for me was that no one really knows what is going on in someone else's brain. Even though

I wanted him to go to the golf course and play, he was quite content to take the lessons and work on his golf swing on the range. That was his passion. Lesson learned—both ways!

※☙☙❧

Handicap Anecdote

HERE'S A LITTLE anecdote that is true and transpired in a golf shop.

The woman behind the front counter was not a golfer and barely knew the basics about golf and all it entailed. She was a student, and the university golf course employed her. She answered the phone and took tee times.

One day, a man came into the shop and said to her, "I want to pay for my handicap."

The female university student looked a bit stunned and appeared to be searching the man for a sign of a "handicap." Finding none, she became perplexed and exasperated. She did not know what the man was talking about. So, she replied, "Just a minute, I'll go get my manager."

❁❁❁❁

Marshmallows for Amateurs

A NEW GOLFER had a lot of tension in her grip and setup. This is not uncommon.

One day, I went over to my teaching "bag of tricks" and pulled out a nice big marshmallow and when the student wasn't looking, I placed the marshmallow on the tee.

When she looked down at the supposed golf ball and instead saw the marshmallow, it loosened her up and she swung without fear and anxiety. The marshmallow helped her relax and helped her much more than my saying, "Relax."

Then she said something to me that was an eye-opener for me. She said, "Oh good, you mean I don't have to be like the pros." She was serious. As it turns out, a lot of amateurs don't want to be like the pros. It is too much pressure. Everyone talks about the pros, and this creates performance anxiety for the average golfer. Because of this, they might never improve. This was a huge obstacle removed for her. It was accomplished through the placement of a nice, big, fat marshmallow on the tee during the lesson.

❦❦❦❦

Finesse Versus Distance

THE FINESSE OF the game is being lost. More and more, as one observes people hitting golf balls on the range, about 80 percent of people are hitting with woods. If one glances over at the short game area and the practice putting green, there are not a lot of golfers practicing at either place.

I have seen people doing the *Happy Gilmore* swing as well. Don't get me wrong, we teaching professionals like to have fun too, but when golfers stand behind the ball and take a run and swing as hard as they can at the ball, they are not really proving anything. It is ok to maybe do it once for fun, but not a whole basket of golf balls!

It seems that distance has become the all-encompassing goal of golf. I believe that golfers would be better off working more on putting and the short game from 80 yards and in. This is where close to 75 percent of the scoring occurs.

I sometimes suggest lightly to the golfer that they should just go play nine holes of golf with a 5-iron, a pitching wedge and a putter. Their score, more than likely, won't be very different than if they used all their clubs. In fact, it might even be better because the golfer will be keeping the ball on the fairway and avoiding trouble.

In addition, let's say you are on the tee box of a daunting 480-yard hole. Your first reaction might be to get overwhelmed with that distance and try to swing as hard as you can at the ball trying to 'kill' it. However, if you take a deep breath, and divide 480 yards by four you come up with 120 yards. So, with four 120-yard shots, you are on the green. Who knows, you might one-putt and get your par. Two-putts gives you a bogey. If you shoot all bogeys and you are a male, you are shooting a bit under what the average male golfer shoots. If you are a female, you are well under what the average female shoots.

What's wrong with that?

Fairway Clubs

I'VE NOTICED THAT for the most part, no one really conquers golf. Instead, golf is the chase of a lifetime. However, if one is patient, has faith, and keeps at the game, there are rewards to be reaped.

One woman was taking a playing lesson from me. She had played some golf, but had never been on the course with a professional. There were many etiquette areas to cover, as well as course management suggestions.

The woman's ball was sitting in the rough, but in a good lie. It was not buried and the woman was over 200 yards from the green and she had her 7-iron out, all set up and ready to hit the ball.

I stopped her and said, "The green is over 200 yards away, why are you using a 7-iron? You need to use a fairway wood."

She looked at me rather quizzically and replied, "A fairway wood? Really? I thought you could only use those on the fairway."

She was thrilled to find this out and of course, it totally changed her long game. The 7-wood is a great club for golfers to use for distance. It is one of the easiest woods to hit. In addition, if the ball is not buried in the rough, it is a good "out of the rough" club when the green is a long way away.

❧❦❧

Nike Clubbing

HERE'S A CONVERSATION I overheard at a golf seminar where there were several stations set up for the ladies to demonstrate golf clubs provided by the various companies.

Two ladies came to the seminar together and one was introducing her friend to another friend who had also showed up at the seminar.

The woman said to the new friend, "And, if you want, we're going clubbing and you're welcome to join us."

The new friend looked around a bit perplexed and replied, "Oh, I do believe the Nike club station is closed now."

Laughing, the other woman replied, "Oh no, I meant we were going night-clubbing, not looking for golf clubs."

❀❀❀

How Could We Forget?

TALK ABOUT FUNNY!

Two ladies were playing golf and got paired with two men. The men hit their tee shots from the white tees and drove down the fairway talking and waiting for the ladies to hit, not paying any particular attention. Shortly, the ladies drove up and they all drove off together to the men's balls on the fairway. The men hit, got back in their carts, and they all drove off again. The women did not seem to be either looking for their balls or anticipating their shots.

So, the men said to them, "Wow, you ladies must have hit really good drives!"

The ladies looked at each other and declared, "Oops, we forgot to hit our drives!"

With that, they turned around and drove back to the tee.

This story points to the fact that women seem to be very social on the golf course.

Sometimes hitting the ball is an afterthought: in this instance, it was not a thought at all!

❧❧❧❧

Toothpicks and Pine Cones

PRACTICE. HOWEVER, PERFECT practice makes perfect! I always tell my students to practice at home and I always provide drills and ways for them to do just that. I tell them 60 repetitions for 21 days will help build a habit. I also tell them they don't necessarily have to hit a golf ball when they practice. Swinging at a tee in the ground or a dandelion or a leaf works well too.

One student returned to her lesson after being given this advice and elatedly told me,

"You would be proud of me, I practiced at home a lot and I practiced swinging at toothpicks."

Another student, after being given this advice, told me she hit pine cones all around her front yard and the neighbors came out and asked her what she was doing. She told them her professional told her to practice her golf swing at home and that is what she was doing!

I love it when my students get creative like this!

❧❧❧❧

Ready, Aim

I ONCE ASKED one of my students where they were aiming, as I usually do.

The student looked up at me and said incredulously, "Oh, I never aim."

And, of course, this brings up the topic of aiming.

I am not going to go into aiming in depth, but I want to speak of it enough that you wonderful golfers know that proper aim is paramount in golf.

I recommend using an intermediate target. This is a small spot (a twig, clump of dirt or such) that is six to eight inches in front of the ball and can be kept in the field of vision when the golfer moves into position to hit the shot.

You must make sure that you get your foot line parallel to the target line.

I cringe when I see the golfer look at the target and proceed to aim their body *at* the target. Of course, this is going to send the ball off to the right for a right-handed golfer and, it might even send it to the left, as the golfer then attempts to compensate.

Please do aim, in life and in golf. Aim. Have a system for aiming. Believe me, your percentages of success are much higher in both arenas if you are careful and attentive in your aim. Precision is paramount and do take time to develop this habit. Repeat it in practice 60 times for 21 days. Then it will be a natural process.

I'll see you down the road if you're aiming the right way!

❧❧❧

Titleists with 380 Dimples

I ALWAYS GET a kick out of the golfer who hasn't been around golf very long and has not taken to the jargon and golf-isms yet.

I linger near the pro shops a lot. One day a woman came running into the pro shop and exclaimed to the assistant professional on duty, "I'd like a box of 'Tit-leists' (with the emphasis on Tit) with 380 dimples."

Of course, the young fellow who was the assistant professional could do nothing but reel for a few seconds. He finally gathered himself and found a box of Titleist golf balls for her. He had to correct her so she wouldn't make the pronunciation mistake again. By the end of that conversation, they were both laughing hysterically.

❧❧

Noon Tee-Time

How ABOUT THE stories that abound of the golfer who calls the pro shop and asks for a tee time around noon? The professional obligingly says, "How about 12:06?"

The caller then replies, "Do you have anything later?"

These two examples really display human nature to me. The game of golf has so many little unknown facts, rituals, and procedures that one can't help but be entertained.

❧❧

Security Blanket

THERE IS THE whole issue of comfort and security in golf. I gave a number of lessons to a woman in California. After a period of time passed, she decided she would take a nine-hole playing lesson from me, so we scheduled it for a few weeks down the road.

In the meantime, this student received a new set of Callaway golf clubs with graphite shafts for her birthday. This was fantastic, because she had an old set of steel shafted, heavy, forged irons that she learned with. She told me in the past that her old 3-iron with the steel shaft was her favorite club to use because the ball went farther. One of the things I had been monitoring was her grip. It was too tight and her fingers would turn red.

The time arrived for the playing lesson. I got the golf cart and loaded up the clubs. As I put the bag of new Callaways onto the cart, I observed there, in the midst of her bag, was her old steel shafted 3-iron. It stood out like a sore thumb. I didn't say anything because I figured she forgot to take it out of her bag.

We arrived at the first tee and she pulled out her driver and hit her drive. Not bad. I hit my drive and we got into the cart. We drove down the fairway and I glanced over at her. There she sat, on the edge of her seat, gripping that old 3-iron! She was really holding it tight. I asked her what she was doing and she said her 3-iron was her security blanket. She proceeded to go over to her ball, still gripping that 3-iron. She hit her shot, got back in the cart, still gripping the 3-iron and said, "Let's go."

I looked at her in puzzlement and she exclaimed, "It's my security blanket, don't you see?"

She proceeded to use that club the whole day whenever she could. I worked my hardest to wean her from it to no avail. More than likely, she probably still carries that 3-iron in the midst of her bag among those gleaming Callaway golf clubs.

Sometimes it is a real challenge for us to get out of our own comfort zones and habitual modes. However, we find that to do so is the only way to improve. Change is difficult. It takes a lot of repetition and belief, and letting go!

❧❧❧❧

Grip Pressure

I ALWAYS HEAR my students say things like:

"I'm gripping the club like I want to strangle it and I have lots of issues."

Whoa! Is this a common refrain or what?

"I'm gripping the club because I don't want to lose it" is another familiar cry!

More often than not, gripping the club too hard is a byproduct of tension and too much thinking. Most golfers aren't aware that they have a death grip on the club. It is rare for a student to self-diagnose too much grip pressure. I believe around 90 percent of golfers are holding the club too tight.

A retired major league pitcher with the San Francisco Giants won over 20 games. He had perfect mechanics, but the ball was flying to the right and to the left of the target. However, his aim was dead on. After observing a number of perfect golf swings and seeing the ball fly off course every time, I knew his grip was too tight. Sure enough, he had a vise-like hold on the club. I mean vise-like. Being a retired major league pitcher, this guy was strong. He was especially holding on tightly with his right hand.

When I explained to lighten the grip and hold it like he preparing to throw a baseball, it registered with him. He striped ball after ball directly at the target. He was almost giddy. I saw renewed life come into his demeanor.

The hands are the only connection to the club. This cannot be over emphasized. All other issues arise from grip pressure. The energy has to flow through the hands into the club itself. If the hands are too tight, they block flow.

Check for grip pressure and reintroduce flow into your golf swing!

Here's another thought regarding grip pressure. Someone once asked Jack Nicklaus what he did to hit the ball farther and he said, "I lighten up my grip." If Jack Nicklaus can do this, so can you.

Once again, less equals more.

❧❧

Quench Wench

I OVERHEARD A woman who drives the beverage cart around the golf course. It was in a southwest desert climate. She was selling cold drinks and beers and beverages to the golfers. After serving the foursome at the tee box she hopped back into her beverage cart, revved the motor, drove off waving and said, "Yup, I call myself Quench Wench."

❧❧

Facebook

THE FOLLOWING IS a testament, of sorts, to our modern society. I had a mixture of people from all walks of life taking group golf lessons together.

When we began introductions at the start of the class, a woman piped up after hearing another woman introduce herself and said,

"Oh, Sally, wow, you're one of my Facebook friends, but this is the first time I've ever met you."

❧❧

7-iron Versus Wood

I AM MOST humored when I recall the question a student asked me. The golfer was a new student, in her 60's, and just beginning to get an idea of the game.

She said, "Pro, could you explain to me exactly when it is that I use a 7-iron and when it is that I use a wood?"

I explained to her the basics of the answer and the main difference between a wood and an iron. She paused, looked at me a bit impishly and exclaimed, "Ah, those details, details. I think I'll just wait and find out."

I reflect back on that moment and I realize it was actually a learning situation more for me than it was for her. Even though I thought I was being comprehensive, there are times when explanations alone will not suffice.

Ah, details, details.

❦❦❦❦

Rusty Golf Shoes

GOLF HAS MANY manifestations. I take great delight in seeing all it has to offer. I note with great humor all the foibles of the current-day golfer.

A man quit the game for six years. One day he told his wife, "I am going to take golf back up again, because I miss it and now I have more time."

She said, "Go right ahead. I know you miss it."

So he put his golf attire and clubs in his car and drove to the driving range. Lots of rust can adhere in six years. He went to his trunk, put on his golf shoes, got his clubs, went to the shop and paid for a bucket of balls. As he walked across the grass to the tee line, something felt amiss. His feet felt funny. He looked down. With shock he realized his old golf shoes were indeed old. His soles came completely out of both shoes. He was walking in his stocking feet. He looked behind him and saw the two leather soles sitting there in the grass where he had walked out of them. This is a true story.

Be sure to check your equipment before you go out to play, especially if you've had a long layoff. This goes for inside your golf bag as well. We all know of many a golfer who put a banana in their golf bag, put the bag away for the season, only to find the banana in the bag in the spring, blackened, hardened and unrecognizable!

Regardless, rust or no rust, banana or no banana, go play golf!

❧❧❧

Parking Brake

SPEAKING OF GOLF humor, here's another. Most people are familiar with the latest and greatest golf pushcarts called speed carts. One of my favorite golfers played a round of golf as usual pushing his speed cart. The whole time, he wondered why it was much harder to push than usual. It didn't seem to be gliding along at the touch of a finger like it usually did.

After the round, this fellow happened to mention this to a buddy in the clubhouse. The buddy, eyeing the golf speed cart, said, "Well, don't you know you've played the whole round with the parking brake on?"

Sure enough, this was the case. The parking brake was engaged the whole 18 holes.

As I reflect upon this bit of humor, I realize there is a lesson here.

How many times do we undertake endeavors where we haven't quite released the parking brake? Or thought we did and didn't? As a consequence, we try harder and expend more effort to obtain much less of a result. All that's necessary is to choose a path, make sure we are on the path, and release the parking brake, i.e. our fears, our mental obstacles, and our efforts. The way can be much easier.

Engaged or disengaged, that is the question.

※☙☙※

Focus and the Owl

FOCUS. YES, THAT seems to be the theme of a really accomplished golfer.

In this day of overstimulation, focus is not an easy task.

Here is a story of how focus and stillness are magnets.

A very good and passionate golfer rose early in the morning before dawn to practice his game on the range. One day, just as the sun was coming up, he knelt down on one knee behind his golf ball. Keeping his body totally still, he stared out to his target and visualized the perfect shot. His stayed motionless as he began to create the shot in his mind.

Suddenly, there was a flash near his knee. He glanced down and unbelievably, there sat a baby...owl! Yes, a baby owl perched on his knee for an instant. Just an instant.

Then, just as suddenly, it flew away.

He told the story to his pals and reflected back on this incident. He thought the only excuse for the owl landing on his knee was the baby owl thought he was a tree because he was so still. The owl hadn't learned all about trees and people yet.

Don't forget this. Be still!

❦❦

Grin and Bear It

TENSION SEEMS TO be the bugaboo of all golfers. I find everyone tensing up their hands, arms and shoulders, and even their facial muscles.

I am going to give you some more tips on how to relax these body parts. Please take this to heart. Your hands are your connection to the club. If they are tense, you are "dead in the water" even before you set foot on the first fairway.

To start it all off, "Grin!"

"What?" you say. "Yes, grin, at address," I say. This will work wonders for you. You can't be tense if you are smiling with your facial muscles.

Now, go ahead and squeeze the club as hard as you can. Yes, that's right, squeeze. Hard.

See. Once you've done that, you've got all that strangling out of your system and your hands are relaxing. This will help immensely. Trust me. I have seen it all.

Practice the grin at all times. Don't you ever wonder why the Dalai Lama is always grinning? Do you see him tense? I don't think he plays golf, but I like the persona he presents. The grin is a slight smile that relaxes the face. Try it. When you are grinning, not much can go wrong on the golf course or in your life.

Grin, and the world grins with you. Frown, and you frown alone.

❧❦❧

Three Men and a Scramble

A GROUP OF three men were preparing to play in their company's scramble tournament. None of them had played golf before. They were eager.

At the end of the series of lessons after they learned putting, chipping, pitching, full swing irons and woods, and course management, they sat down with a beer and said to me,

"We've been talking and came up with a great idea. This game is lots more difficult than we originally thought. How about if we pay you to play in the tournament for us and we'll sit in the clubhouse and drink beer and wait for you to finish on our behalf?"

Everyone, of course, found this very funny. But they were seriously considering alternatives to playing in the scramble, as they found the game a bit daunting.

In the end, they decided to play in the tournament themselves. I thought this was a testament to their fortitude. I knew they had undergone an intense learning process. I also knew they were trying hard as well. Some things just take time.

❧❧❧

Why Rush Things?

GOLFERS DO SAY the most far-fetched things at times.

There is a golfer who keeps the plastic on her woods. She plays with the plastic on and it is all snagged and dirtied. I said to her, "Oh, you've still got the plastic on, I see."

She replied, "Yes, why rush things?"

❧❧❧

The Goal in Golf

THERE WAS A new golfer taking a pitching lesson for the first time. She had two previous lessons on grip and setup and a putting lesson. She was trying to hit over a bunker and she said, "What's really the goal here?

I replied, "Have you ever seen golf played on television or elsewhere?"

"No," she replied. "I really don't know what is supposed to happen. Am I supposed to hit the ball into the sand trap?"

I told her to go and watch golf on television to see what to do. She's just not sure what to do in golf. One wonders why she didn't do a little golf background research before signing up for lessons.

This goes to show us that we can't make even the basest of assumptions with people in golf and in life. We never really know what is in a person's head unless we ask.

❦❦❦❦

Humor From the Mouths of Golfers

A GOLFER WAS overheard exclaiming after a number of practice swings in preparation to hit the ball, "Oh, I'm afraid I'm going to 'topple' the ball!"

❦❦❦❦

One-Iron

ONE GOLFER CARRIES a one-iron in her bag for fun. She thinks that one day she will make a hole-in-one with it!

❀❧❧❀

Incredible

ONE GOLFER WAS told by another golfer that he had a hole-in-one. She replied, "What is that?"

❀❧❧❀

Social Climbing

A GOLFER AT a one-day seminar told this story that occurred at her private club in California.

A woman came up to her and said, "You know Leona, at this club, people aren't judged anymore on their economic status. They're judged on their golf handicap."

Leona did not know what to say. She is a real estate investor and has a Masters in social work, as well as being a sculptor.

So, she said nothing and went on about her business.

❧❦❧

Gone To Pot

A LADY CALLED for golf lessons. She is 69. She wants to play more golf and improve. She's not had lessons and her granddaughter is helping her.

"My granddaughter helps me more than my son-in-law does—he's a 'know it all.'" said the grandmother.

Anyway, she went to play, hit the driver, and rammed it into the ground and got a bump the size of a grapefruit on her hand. She thought she broke something, so she went for an x-ray. She hoped taking lessons would prevent any more injuries of this kind.

So, she and her 16-year old granddaughter began the lessons. It might have been my imagination, but I smelled marijuana on the grandmother during a couple of lessons. I thought, hmm…this student is smoking marijuana to relax with golf, and she's a grandmother. The smell was unmistakable.

I guess this is not hard to believe, because people have a hard time relaxing, and golf is challenging. I don't think the granddaughter was aware of all this. I zoomed in on a crazy picture in my mind of the grandmother with a joint at home in her rocker, getting ready for the lesson!

❧❧❧

Appearances Are Important

HUMAN NATURE IS visible in golf. Who knew that when golf began in Scotland it would evolve to the level it has with all the equipment, golf courses, books, golfers, and a whole industry surrounding it.

I still love the little vignettes that tell of golfers and their mindset and give us a window on human nature.

To wit:

There is a very successful lady who works in real estate in a medium-sized town. She is VERY well known about town. She carries her clubs in her car trunk as she drives around, BUT she doesn't play golf. However, she says she is a golfer because she carries her clubs in her trunk. I guess she sells more real estate that way.

❧❧❧

Free Lessons by Osmosis

ANOTHER WOMAN TOOK a series of lessons. At the end of one of the lessons, she said to me,

"So, my husband has sure improved since I've been taking lessons from you."

As it turns out, he would wait at the door after each of her lessons. He made her sit down and tell him every single thing I said during the lessons. Then, he went out and tried it all on the driving range and golf course and showed marked improvement.

❧❧❧

An Incidental

ONE COMMENT I make quite often to the student is as follows:

"The ball is an incidental, don't focus on the ball."

This always manages to create a look of surprise. For many, this is a new concept. After all, they've been told how important the ball is.

They say, "Well, what am I supposed to focus on, since all the information I read tells me that I need to focus on the ball?"

Focusing on the ball causes undue tension and the target becomes least important in a person's mind. This is counter-productive.

Then I say, "You know all the energy you are putting on the ball?"

"Yes," they reply.

I say, "You need to put that energy on the target. You can look at the ball, but don't stare at it so intently. This creates tension and interferes with flow."

"Oh," replies the student. "I never thought of that!"

This little tidbit of information sometimes revolutionizes their complete golf game.

And, in golf, what is more important than the TARGET?

This is just one more little thing to remember, right?

One-Liners

I JUST LOVE some of the one-liners I hear golfers exclaiming.
I want to share a few of them with you.

My driving and hybrids have gone
to hell in a hand basket.

I drive like I putt.

If you can get me into striking distance
at age 56, you've accomplished a lot.

I have a very bad idea of how I need to contort.

I've been a 'hit and miss' golfer
for quite some time now.

My hybrids are my 'chopping' clubs.

I think I would be 'hee-hawed' off the course
without knowing the bare essentials.

I would like to get to where I could think
about strategy, but right now, I'm too busy
thinking about how to hit the ball. I think
I need to simplify in my mind.

I played in the Peace Corps in Ecuador many years ago. Some friends' parents gave me 3 bags, 30 clubs, and 1000 golf balls to get me started.

❦❧

Tee Art

SO MANY GOLFERS are creative and creativity is an integral part of the game.

One woman was taking a golf lesson and I used colored tees to tee up each ball. This way the student can experience success. It gives them a good lie.

The poor woman kept topping the ball. She drove the tee into the ground such that she and I couldn't retrieve it. We left it there and used a different tee each time.

After about ten of these topped shots and each colored tee going into the ground and leaving an array of colors, the student exclaimed, "Oh, look, tee art!"

"Yes, I replied smiling at the pretty pattern, "We could probably draw dot-to-dot here. We have a very colorful design developing with all these colored tees in the ground!"

❧❧❧

Color Blind

I WAS DOING the same thing in another lesson. Many times, I will have the student swing at the tee in the ground first as this relieves tension. There's no ball and the student relaxes. I told the student to swing at the beige tee I put in the ground. He exclaimed, "I can't swing at it because I can't see it. I'm color blind."

That was an eye-opener for me. It was another reminder that communication is so imperative in golf lesson interaction.

❧❧❧

Paralysis by Analysis

TOO MANY GOLFERS are analyzing their shots ad infinitum.

I say to everyone who takes a lesson from me, "Don't analyze the game while you are playing the game."

The majority of golfers, after a poor hit, will ask, "Why did I do that?"

This question should not be asked at all during play. It should be saved for afterwards. After the golf game is the appropriate time to analyze. This kind of training is difficult for the average golfer. In their desire to conquer the game and hit a great shot every time, they slow their progress by analyzing when they are supposed to be playing.

The reason I suggest no analyzing during play is because it sends the golfer into the left side of their brain. This is not wrong, but it is the side of the brain that is not accustomed to *playing*. The right side of the brain is the playing side. This is where the golfer wants to be while *playing* golf.

The idea in golf is to hit the ball, find it, and hit it again. Why are we making this so difficult? We must forget the analyzing until later. We must try to play like a child plays. Children just *play*. They don't *think* about playing. The experience of playing brings us into the present moment. The present moment is where the action is.

C'mon. If not now, when? That is the question. Now is your chance. Forget about "how to." Just go "do it" as the ads say. What are you waiting for? You might just surprise yourself.

❧❧

Alignment/Linemen

HUMOR CAN BE the best medicine.

A mother and daughter took group lessons with me. I mentioned aiming and said that today the group would be working on alignment.

The daughter took lessons when she was eight years old and she's 22 now. I asked the group, "Who knows what "alignment" is?"

The daughter quickly raised her hand and said,

"Yes, I know, it's that group of men that protect the quarterback!"

❧❧

Mis Madres

HERE'S ONE FOR those of you who speak a bit of Spanish.

Another lady in another group lesson said, "No puedo golpear mis madres." She repeated it again in Spanish for fun.

Then, we laughed and she and I (since I speak a bit of Spanish) realized she meant "No puedo golpear mis maderas."

The difference is madres means mothers, and maderas means woods. So, she was saying, "I can't hit my mothers!"

Madres, maderas, oh my.

❧❧❧

Hop with your Left Foot

LOTS OF GOLFERS have many talents and different skill levels. It is up to me to discover the background of the students as well as whether they play other sports, are left- or right-handed and so forth.

One day, the following occurred:

I asked, "Are you left- or right-handed?"

The student replied, "I hop with my left foot, look with my left eye and I bat right-handed."

I had never heard this question answered this way before. This is one of the reasons I kept teaching golf for 22 years. I was simply amazed on a daily basis. I still am and always will be and I love it.

Right, left, right, left.

❧❧❧

Poet Laureate Plays Golf

DURING SIX OF my teaching years, I traveled to Tucson, Arizona in the winter. I taught golf and renewed and recharged my spirit. Part of this spirit renewal and recharge came in pursuing volunteer work at a special place, the University of Arizona Poetry Center. I love poetry and writing. I volunteered there and was asked to help put a poetry project together for a computer program.

I worked on permissions and I loved delving into the stacks and pulling out the poetry books. I also helped at readings the Poetry Center hosted. The staff was so appreciative and kind to me. They always invited me to the poetry readings and functions hosted by the Center. They treated me like their biggest donor.

One weekend in March the former national poet laureate of the United States, Billy Collins, came to Tucson as the keynote speaker for a local writer's group. He had time on his hands, and the staff asked me to join Billy on the golf course with two other board members. Billy is quite a golf aficionado. The staff wanted to make sure he enjoyed his time in Tucson and got to play a great golf course.

Our game was scheduled for early morning. The temperatures had dropped the previous night and we faced a frost delay. I arrived at the course and went into the restaurant where we were to meet. When I walked in and met Billy, I immediately felt a soul connection—maybe it was because we both loved golf, and were Irish and loved poetry. I saw the glint in his eye and that's all I needed to know that this was a special man.

We sat and talked and drank our coffee and finally it was time to get out on the golf course. The day turned glorious with great temperature, great camaraderie, and great scenery. We were all enjoying our individual games and having great conversation. Billy had a nice grasp of the game and how to play. Not many do. Towards the end of the round, Billy came over to me and said, "Annie, if you were to give me one piece of advice about my golf swing, what would it be?"

I said, without missing a beat, "Well, Billy, you need to put a comma at the top of your backswing."

A moment passed and Billy burst into laughter as he assimilated exactly what I meant.

"Well said," he exclaimed.

That is the story that christened me "Poetry Center Golf Professional."

The Poetry Center staff loves to tell this story when the occasion arises.

That night, after Billy gave his keynote speech and read his poetry to the appreciative crowd, he returned to the table and commented to me, "You inspired me, Ann—watching you today do your thing on the golf course inspired me doing mine, so thank you."

As my Irish grandmother would say to me when I was growing up, "We are lucky, Irish and blessed, Ann."

❧❧❧

Swishing Flagstick

ONE TIME I was playing golf in Phoenix with a friend and we got paired with two guys. One just happened to be Rick Sutcliffe, the Chicago Cubs baseball pitcher. The Cubs were in Phoenix for spring training and many took to the local golf courses whenever they could. Rick brought along one of his buddies this day. They were very adequate players, and, quite the golf course jesters.

I remember that they were having tons of fun and chiding each other at every turn. About halfway into the round, Rick's buddy stood over his putt, lining it up and was ready to make the stroke. Just as he took the putter back and proceeded to make contact, sly Rick, standing behind him, took the flagstick, held it like a bat on the non-flag end, and made the hardest baseball swing he could over his friend's back as he attempted to putt.

The sound of a swinging and whooshing flag was like a jetliner surging overhead. The buddy about fell over. He proceeded to whack the ball way across the green. When he turned to see what possibly could have made the noise and realized it was Rick, he laughed. They both got hysterical, especially Rick, and from that point on, we all paid extra attention to where Rick stood when we putted! We just weren't sure of what "surprises" Rick might come up with.

❧❧

The Pro Survives

GOLF, MAYBE BECAUSE of its complicated nature and its intensity, seems to lend itself to foibles and escapades.

I was giving an afternoon golf lesson. It was a bright, sunshiny day and I was wearing my sunglasses. Thank goodness. The student was hitting range balls off a mat and I was standing, facing him, about two feet away from the ball. He took a hefty swing and actually hit underneath the ball that was sitting on a rubber tee. In slow motion, the ball came up in the air, straight at me. I could see it coming, but in reality, it was all happening so fast that I couldn't react. Sure enough, the ball hit me squarely between the eyes on the bridge of my nose. But I had my sunglasses on, so there was no harm done, and no injury.

Another time, I was teaching a small group lesson. The hitting area on the range was marked by two yellow ropes stretched from end to end. This is where the golfers stood to hit their golf balls. I stepped up to one student in the group and arranged his arms in the backswing motion. I backed away so he could take a swing.

Lo and behold, before I knew it, I was falling down backwards with my visor flying off. I caught my foot on the yellow rope just enough for it to trip me up. It was a helpless feeling. I recall slowly falling to the ground and laying there flat on my back, with no visor. All I could do was laugh and act nonchalant as I got up, dusted myself off, replaced my visor and went to work with the next student.

Both of these incidents are etched in my brain. What occurred was out of my control. I had to just give in and get hit and fall down. It reminded me to pay attention and stay alert, even though I realize that sometimes that may not be enough.

❦❧❦❧

Playing Through

A FRIEND OF mine was playing with his regular group of buddies. They came upon a foursome of ladies on a par three. The ladies were not moving along expeditiously. They hit their tee shots on the par three and were chatting up a storm. There was some extra room between the ladies and the group ahead who were already on the next hole. The women waved the group of buddies up and said, "Why don't you play through here?"

The buddies agreed and they hit their shots and began walking to the green. They noticed the ladies were now hurrying up which they thought a bit odd. However, they continued on up to the green. They arrived at the green, only to see the ladies there ahead of them and hitting their shots.

The buddies exclaimed, "We thought you wanted us to play through?"

The ladies looked at them, smiled and exclaimed, "Yes, we did, but we got here first!"

✿❧❧✿

Toupee Divot

I PLAY WITH a very good golfer and friend of mine named Printer. He and I talk about the meaning of golf. We discuss golf's obstacles and challenges. He possesses fantastic wisdom and can laugh easily as he understands irony.

One day he and I were playing golf with his son. It was a glorious fall day in Missoula, Montana, where nature is magnified. The glint of sunshine on the leaves, the multi-colored landscape of sky, mountains, grass, and trees had us all relishing our day on the links.

His son was riding in my cart. We stopped to watch Printer hit an iron shot. Printer made a beautiful swing that produced a large perfectly formed divot. Printer held his follow through. As we watched, the nicely formed divot hung on the club and then flew up into the air. Then, kerplunk! It landed on top of Printer's head and sat there like a toupee. Printer looked over at us, somewhat befuddled, put his hand on top of his head and felt the chunk of grass sitting there. We all got giddy with laughter.

Finally, he took the divot and replaced it perfectly back into the ground. This put a little smile on our faces for the remainder of the round. When we finished our game, we rehashed the "divot on the head" incident. I jokingly asked Printer if he had performed magic acts in another lifetime. He replied, "No, no, but I'm not sure even Siegfried and Roy could have duplicated this divot act today."

This might have been even more exciting than seeing a hole-in-one!

❀❧❧❀

Bagged Ball

THIS STORY COMES from a friend of mine out of Cherokee, Iowa, on the 9-hole course I grew up on. There were and still are many evenings where the kids can go out and play golf and have a great time. There is no rush and no hurry and they can play at their own pace.

A friend of mine named Jane went home to visit her sister, Mary, in Cherokee. They decided to play a few holes of golf after dinner. By the time they arrived on the eighth tee box, it was getting very dark and they couldn't see the tee shots. There was a group of kids leaving the eighth green and heading to the ninth tee box nearby as they approached. Mary and Jane yelled to the kids that they were going to tee off. The kids stopped and bent down and hid behind their small junior golf bags. Mary hit her shot. She and Jane couldn't see, but they heard a clunk followed by one of the boys excitedly crying out, "Hey, it's in the bag!"

Yup, Mary hit her tee shot directly into the boy's small junior golf bag. From what Jane tells me, the boys were very impressed and were in awe that Mary performed this amazing feat!

❧❧❧

Golf and the Pyramids

THE PRO SHOP, the driving range, the clubs, the bags, the balls and many things about golf can be intimidating to someone who hasn't been educated on its procedures. I have a good friend who runs programs for Girl Scouts in Montana. She recounted her first foray to the driving range at a very nice resort. All the range balls were piled pyramid style, as they sometimes are for presentation and appearances only.

My friend told me she thought the pyramids were very nice and she began to hit. She figured it was going to take forever to hit all those balls. Yes, she thought she had to hit every last ball in the pyramid. No one told her otherwise.

So, she proceeded to do just that. She had to hit fast, though, because it was a warm-up for her game. She was to tee off in 15 minutes. She did manage to hit the whole pyramid, but obviously, was worn out for her round of golf!

❧❧❧

Peruvian Hawks

ANOTHER FRIEND OF mine is the head professional in Great Falls, Montana. She recounts the story of the big flock of Peruvian hawks that come every year for a couple of months and circle over the golf course. Unfortunately, these are prime golf months. These Peruvian hawks like to swoop down and peck at unsuspecting people's cap-less heads as they play.

People have to wave their clubs at the hawks and really be aggressive to get the hawks to fly away.

As my friend says, "I hope these hawks return to Peru soon, because it's a challenge. We have one man who couldn't move fast enough to escape a swooping bird, and he's ok, but the top of his head looks like a Chinese puzzle!"

❦❦❦

Bunker Mentality

ONE OF MY students hit his ball into a sand bunker that had a pretty good-sized lip. He made a swing at the sand to get out, the ball hit the lip, came back and hit him in the chest and fell into the bunker again. On try number two, same thing. He hit the sand; the ball flew into the lip, flew back and hit him in the chest, and fell back into the bunker. On try number three, yes, you got it, same thing. On try number four, he finally mercifully managed to get out and the ball landed on the green. However, he had to add his penalty strokes for the ball hitting him, and now he was on the green, but he had a very long 30-foot putt.

Oh heck, he thought in disgust, and stood over the ball, and just putted it. What happens? You got it—lo and behold, the ball rolls the 30 plus feet and drops smack dab into the cup!

Once again, golf, after putting the golfer through a multitude of crazy scenarios, rewards him with the thrill of making a very long and seemingly unmakeable putt. Who knew? Who knows? Who could know? Our only option seems to be to keep on playing!

❧❧❧

Golf Armor

As I've mentioned before, a lot of my students take me literally when I say something. This always put a smile on my face.

Every season, I teach a series of group lessons. The sequence of five lessons goes from putting to chipping to pitching to full swing to full swing woods. One day at the close of a pitching lesson, I said jokingly, "Ok, people, be sure to put on your armor next week, as we will be working on full swing."

A student immediately approached me and said seriously, "Well, where do we get that?"

As I reflect back on this humorous incident, I realize that there is so much equipment in the golf industry, that golfers are overwhelmed. There are bags and balls and tees and clubs and ball markers and hats and visors and shoes and gloves, etc. One might understand why a new golfer would ask this question. It all kind of makes sense. Plus, she probably heard that golfers yelled "fore" a lot and she wanted to be prepared.

ஐஜஜஐ

Rita Hayworth
and James Garner

MANY TIMES THE golf shop will book golf lessons for me. I leave my lesson book there so they can do so. One Friday I was finishing up lessons, but had one more to give. I looked at my book and the name of the student was Rita Hayworth. I thought how cool that I'm giving a lesson to someone with a famous movie star's name.

The next day, I'm at the range, ready to give my first lesson and I look at the name in the book and it's James Garner, another famous movie star. What a rare coincidence. I thought maybe someone was pulling the wool over my eyes. Of course, neither person was the real actor or actress, but it made for a fun conversation with them when I told them the story. Once again, it relaxed them and put them in a receptive mood for their lesson.

❀❧❀

Putting or Putting?

THIS STORY WAS born from a group putting lesson I gave one week as a part of the series. The following week after the putting lesson, one of the women in the group returned to take the chipping lesson and told me she had something to share with me. She said that she diligently made a list one evening last week of the things she had to do the next day. She included "practice putting" on the list.

The next day, she picked up the to do list, read down it and came to "practice putting." Hmm, she said to herself, "practice putting." Hmm, she thought. Gee, I wonder what I am supposed to practice putting away?

It finally dawned on her, but not right away. She had to rack her brain to figure out what she was supposed to practice putting…away. She was befuddled. She knew I would get a kick out of the story. I did. We shared it with the whole class. They howled with laughter. She was a good sport to tell about her gaffe.

But, hey, this is a funny game, right?

❧❧❧

Sorority Sisters

EVERY YEAR, I return to my alma mater, the University of Iowa, to teach a golf clinic and play nine holes with my Kappa Kappa Gamma sorority sisters. We have done this for over 15 years. Some of the women are golfers and some only play once per year at this clinic. We laugh and it is truly a load of fun. Often, various sorority sisters float in and out, attending when they can through the years. There is a core group that attends every year.

Recently, I received a phone call from a Kappa sister months after the clinic. She said, "You really helped me in the Kappa golf clinic. I've been taking lessons since then, and now I have about 12 things to think about on my back swing. I want you to know that I have come up with something on my own to think about. I just can't think of all of those 12 things when I swing.

She said, "I say to myself turn tall and let it fall. How do you like that, Ann?"

I told her that she had done the right thing, as she was able to morph all the information into a phrase that worked for her!

I often refer to this in my mind because I think this is a good example of teachers providing too much information. The student goes on overload. She was somehow able to compress this technical information into one simple phrase that worked for her. This is another good example of less equals more.

❧❧❧

Same Golf Ball

THERE WAS ANOTHER Kappa clinic where I brought nice new Titleist pink-ribboned golf balls and gave one to each Kappa. Lo and behold, we were playing a scramble and everyone hit and we played with six in a group. I was alternating back and forth between the two groups.

As it turned out, everyone in each group used their new ball with the pink ribbon on it. They were running around asking me, "Is that my ball?" It was total chaos.

❧❧❧

Bags Falling

I THINK IT was the same year that one of the members in the Kappa group took off from number one tee box in a cart at a high rate of speed. Her golf bag fell off the cart onto the fairway. She had not used the belt to fasten it. She was clueless, kept on driving, got to her ball and wondered where her clubs were. When she looked back down the fairway, there they were, lying in a heap, with everyone doubled over with laughter.

❧❧❧

Red or White Tees?

I WAS PLAYING golf in California with another LPGA professional friend of mine at a public course. We were paired with two fellows, one a policeman and the other a physical trainer. On the first tee, the policeman said, "Which tees are you playing from?"

My friend and I said the white tees and we proceeded to play. We had a lot of fun and one of the guys even signed up for lessons.

When my friend and I went into the pro shop afterward to thank the staff for the round, the counter person smiled and told us they told the two men we were playing with at the start that we were golf professionals. They said the men didn't believe them. However, at the turn, the two men stopped in to use the restroom, and stopped by the pro shop and said, "We didn't believe they were pros, but we believe it now."

My friend and I thought this was a very cute story!

However, some interesting things also happen when I get paired up, being a female professional. One time, when I was playing with the same LPGA friend, we got sent as a twosome out to the first tee. There was a group of four men at the tee ready to tee off. We asked them if we could go ahead since we were a twosome and the fairway ahead was open. They begrudgingly said yes, and they did not seem pleased to be sending a twosome of "women" out ahead of them.

We proceeded to go toward the white tees, and immediately one exclaimed, "You ladies are supposed to hit from the red tees." And then the buddy said, "I've never seen a woman hit from the white tees."

I teed up my ball at the white tee box and said with a smile, "Well, our swings are the same regardless of what tee we hit from." I said it nicely.

My friend and I hit, and as we took off we heard one of them murmur, "Oh, they have beautiful swings."

They eventually caught up to us later in the round when play slowed. They saw our LPGA bag tags and one of them called the next day and asked if he could take lessons. He told us that he wanted to swing like we did!

❦❧❦

Another Tee Story

ANOTHER TIME I was practicing for a tournament while living in Austin, Texas. I went to play by myself so I could practice. However, I was paired with another man. After the pleasantries, I headed toward the white tees to hit.

He immediately piped up with, "You're supposed to hit from the red tees."

I said, "I think I'll just try one from here."

I proceeded to stripe one down the fairway about 240 yards and he said, in awe, "Oh, you must be a professional."

It was very cute and it's rather interesting how the tee boxes are viewed. We really need to have people teeing off on certain tee boxes according to their handicap or scoring level rather than their gender. Some golf courses (very few) have introduced this idea. The golfer reports their handicap or scoring average to the front desk when they check in. They then are instructed which tees to hit from. This makes sense and allows people to play within their capacities while still being challenged. It would speed up play because people would not be playing from the "tips" all the time.

❧❧

Tee Markers

SPEAKING OF TEES, I actually saw a person place a ball on the tee marker thinking that they were supposed to hit the ball off the tee marker for their first shot. Crazy!

❦❦

High-Centered

I once accompanied a group of golfers from California to Sedona, Arizona.

I was in a golf cart taking pictures and video and moving from group to group. I was on the tee box of a par three hole and I was waiting to photograph the group teeing off.

All of a sudden, the group on the green looked back and saw me and they began waving and shouting loudly, "She's on a boulder, she's on a boulder." They were agitated.

I thought, well, that's not a problem; she can just take a penalty stroke. I yelled back, "Just tell her to take an unplayable lie."

"No, no." they responded. "Her golf cart is on the boulder."

I looked a bit more closely, and sure enough, one of the women had driven off to the side of the cart path in search of her ball. There were a lot of rocks and boulders in that area and she drove over one big boulder and became "high-centered."

The cart wheels were spinning in mid-air. She was sitting in the driver's seat pushing on the accelerator rather panicked. The cart's underneath mid-section was stuck on the boulder! She was going nowhere fast. Eventually, they were able to dislodge the cart and finish the round.

❧❧❧❧

Lahinch First Tee

FOR FIVE YEARS in a row, a client hired me to teach her golf for two weeks. The fun part of this was she wanted to learn on the great links courses in Ireland.

If anyone has played links courses, you know how challenging they can be. This woman was a highly successful lawyer and had great focus. This would serve to her benefit as she continued to "stay the course" of instruction for those five years on the Ireland trips.

She just focused until she got it.

The first year, we scheduled Lahinch in County Clare in western Ireland. My friend would indeed meet a challenge here. I really should have started her on a par three course, but she insisted on the links courses in Ireland! Ok, we could manage this.

We proceeded to the first tee. It was between the clubhouse and the pro shop. There were people looking out the windows from both places. It is rare to see a female professional play golf in Ireland.

My friend became very nervous when it was her turn to hit. All of a sudden she realized the enormity of the fact that here she was, playing links golf, and she had barely played 18 holes before. Luckily, it was wintertime, so the course was not crowded and we could take our time. Thank goodness for that. She walked to the tee box and, barely breathing, placed her tee into the ground. Then, she attempted to place her ball on the tee—well, who would think this would be a challenge? She could not get the ball to stay on the tee for the life of her!

She tried maybe four or five more times. I got a bit dizzy with laughter, but I knew I had to hold it in, because everyone was watching. She was smiling too, and trying to hold back her laughter. I was silently praying for her!

We both knew she needed to perform. She was on the edge of not doing so. We both could picture the "locals" looking at us from the windows and wondering what the heck this "yahoo" American was doing. How hard could it be to at least get a ball onto a tee?

Finally, and with great emphasis on the word finally, she got the ball to balance on the tee. It seemed it took an eternity. But, she had only begun. Now, she had to hit her drive. Oh dear.

Still weakened from the whole teeing up the ball experience and holding back the laughter, she took a mighty swing. I was standing nearby still praying!

"Aargh," emanated from her mouth. She almost lost her balance. We both were speechless as her ball popped up in the air and landed barely 10 feet from the front of the tee box. Rather unceremoniously, she bent over, picked up her tee, and slunk off the tee box walking forward to hit her next shot. I followed her. Neither of us looked to either window to see what the Irish faces were doing. We just couldn't bear it. We moved forward with speed, as we knew that the leprechauns had, indeed, pulled one over on us. And, we assumed there was more to come!

Now, whenever my friend and I play, we grin as we go to any number one tee box in Ireland. She has come a long way from that first day with her advancement in golf, having played some of Europe's most challenging courses including Royal County Down, Royal Portrush and Ballybunion.

❧❧❧❧

Wal-Mart Pros

ONE DAY I was having lunch and waiting for my LPGA friend to finish giving her lesson at the range. I was seated next to a couple of fellows who were watching her teach. One of the men said to the other, "Why don't you take a few classes in golf and you can get a job teaching golf and then you wouldn't have to work at Wal-Mart?"

Can you believe that? Some of the general public has no idea. Becoming a certified LPGA/PGA golf professional takes at least four years minimum. After that, it takes years of observation and experience before one really rises to the top of golf instruction. About all I could do with this comment was sit back in amazement and chuckle!

❧❧❧❧

Three-Club Tournament

ANOTHER CONVERSATION I overheard as I was sitting eating lunch went as follows:

"I'm playing in a three-club tournament this weekend," said one golfer to another.

"Oh," replied the other golfer, "Which three clubs? Is one of them this course?"

"No," grinned the first golfer, "It's a four-hybrid, a six-iron, and a nine-iron."

Again, communication and interpretation come into play here. No wonder the world at large is in such confusion.

❦❦❦

Shadowy Spine Angle

IT WAS A bright, sunny summer day and I was finishing up a lesson with two female golfers who were relatively new to the game. It was around 6:00 pm. One of the golfers was having trouble maintaining her spine angle throughout her swing and she kept topping the ball or hitting behind it. I explained to her that she needed to maintain her posture throughout her swing. We tried a number of ways to do this. Today was a day I could use my favorite drill for this particular problem because of the sun and its shadow. I put a club on the ground at the top of her shadow in front of her.

I laid the club parallel to the target line at the top of her shadow, so she could watch it throughout the swing. This way she would be able to see when she came out of her posture. She would see the shadow go above the club lying on the ground.

She got excited, and exclaimed, "Can I do this at home?"

I said yes, but she would need another person to set the club on the ground. "Oh yes," she replied. "And, exactly how far away from my body should it be?"

I replied, "I don't know, it all depends on the time of day."

We paused, thought about this, and laughed. We realized that shadows grew smaller or larger, depending on the time of day. It was a very funny conversation. It lightened her up and helped her relax. For the rest of the lesson, she maintained her posture and now had a visual picture to follow.

The discovery of these things during a lesson makes the lesson rewarding for me. A good instructor has to be sure they pay attention. There are nuances and adaptations that must be considered.

❦❧

Don't Use your Woods

ONE OF MY students was told during her lessons 25 years ago to never use her woods. She said to me, "And here it is, 25 years later, and I still haven't used my woods." She was serious. That is a long time to play golf and never hit a wood!

❦❧

This Is Kind of Fishy

I HAVE HAD two students bring me fish as a thank you for lessons. One came carrying a bucket of ice, filled with fresh salmon from the Pacific Coast of California—when I was teaching golf there. The other brought me fresh halibut from his fishing trip up to Alaska!

❦❦❦

Backing Into the Barn

DURING GOLF SCHOOL one year in San Jose, California, we had a great guest instructor. It was a hot summer day. We asked her to explain and demonstrate the posture and setup to the group of 16 gathered round. As the guest instructor went through a wonderful explanation of posture and setup, she began to demonstrate. She turned her backside to the group, bent over, and said, "See, it's just like a cow backing into a barn," and she backed up, rear end first, towards the group.

It was a rather startling demonstration, given the fact that she had on white shorts and as she backed up, her polka dot underwear was clearly visible through the shorts! I think the ladies thought it was all planned out, as they began to laugh a bit, murmur, and look fleetingly at each other. But, no, we all soon realized that our guest instructor had no idea what was going on until we told her later on in the day over a cocktail. Of course, she was horrified.

❄❧❧❄

Student Statements

HERE ARE SOME actual statements from my students:

I played my best when I was five months pregnant.

I never keep score and I play a lot better.

If you're lost in the desert or mountains,
carry a golf club and start swinging it.

I am going to play golf with
30 other loggers tomorrow.

I won a driver for the shortest drive my
first time out in a scramble golf tournament.

I was going to my hotel room with my
clubs and coming out of the elevator with
my bag. I struggled with it and all the
clubs spilled out all over the elevator,
just as the door was closing.

No one has been this nice to me before.

I swing at dandelions and call them Marguerite
—I'm half French.

I'm a former gymnast, but I can't
do handsprings anymore.

My husband is called Divot Dave
and he's the one who packs my clubs.

I get close to the green and I fall apart.

The inside-outside swing means nothing to me.

I've been teeing up the ball in the fairway
and hitting my driver. We recently played
in Mexico and I teed it up in the fairway
and my caddy yelled, "No, no señora!" My husband
told him, "Let her do what she wants to do!"

I'm a "pre-beginner" or whatever
level comes before beginner.

I am saying "no" to everything but golf.

I am currently playing hack and chase.

I am taking lessons because I don't
want to hit too many people in the head.

My husband told me to take lessons so
I don't end up like all the other golfers.

❧❧❧

Foxy Golfer

THERE IS A family of foxes that makes its residence at one of the courses where I teach in Montana. The national news came and filmed the mother fox running out to the fairway from the rough and taking the golf ball in her mouth and running away with it. No one has found the stash, but she must have hundreds of balls, as she has been doing this since the course opened a couple of years ago!

One day, I was playing golf there and my ball went into a bunker. I got my sand wedge and descended into the bunker towards my ball. Out of the corner of my eye I saw something coming at me through the bunker from the other side. I stopped. It was a fox going after my ball! All of a sudden, it came after **me**. It charged, stopped, stepped back, and then grabbed the ball in its mouth and raced off. Another victory.

By the way, does anyone know the rule here?

✿✿✿

Cubs and Cows

MONTANA BEING MONTANA, it does have its share of animals that roam around and sometimes get into residential areas.

One day, the police were called to the golf course to sedate a small black bear cub who had become separated from its mother. The golfers calmly continued hitting balls on the range as the bear cub ran across the middle of the driving range and climbed up a tree and sat there.

Another day, the police were called to subdue a runaway cow. Yes, that's right, a runaway cow at the golf course. It must have jumped out of a cattle truck that was passing by. It ran into the golf parking lot and began to circle. No one knew what to do.

The police came and a comedy of errors ensued as seven policemen desperately tried to usher this bovine runaway back into a truck. It put a new meaning to the term "cattle drive," that's for sure!

The funniest thing was the looks on the golfers' faces as they drove into the parking lot for their round of golf!

❧❧

Raven Thieves

ONE SEASON, I worked in a golf shop as an assistant in Montana. The club was situated not far from the immense Bob Marshall Wilderness Area. The BMWA is the largest roadless wilderness in the United States, and people have to pack in on horses.

Many times we would have locals come by the golf shop and report on friends who trekked back into the wilderness on overnight camping trips. They found golf balls nestled in the grass way back miles into the wilderness and couldn't figure out how they got there.

Once again, the ravens were gathering shiny golf balls from the driving range. They flew off with them for miles and dropped them into the wilderness area. The hikers found brand new Callaways, Titleists and Nikes in places where few people had ever been.

❧❧❧

Squirrels

THEN THERE'S THE story of the squirrel at the golf course. He has been fed one too many times and jumps into golf carts. He grabs people's chips and sandwiches. The staff finally named this one Hal, as he even came into the shop on more than one occasion to check things out.

One of the members contributed to this squirrel problem. I saw the member arrive at the practice area carrying a wooden box with something inside. He set the box down, opened the side of it, and out hopped a squirrel. He said he didn't like squirrels in his yard, so he's been trapping them and bringing them to the golf course. He releases them so they can be with all the other squirrels. Hmm…

❀❀❀

Look Where?

KATHLEEN WAS A brand new golfer. I was working with her on her backswing. I proceeded to take her to the top of her backswing where we stopped and I said, "Look."

She raised her head and looked all around, rather perplexed and said, "Where am I supposed to look?"

This was another learning experience for me. She really didn't understand the process of what we were doing in the lesson, and I had assumed she did. It was funny to see her looking all around—everywhere except at her backswing position!

❀❀❀

What's Supposed to Happen Here?

AND, BELIEVE IT or not, I had a student who had never played or watched golf. She said to me at her first lesson, "What's supposed to happen here? Is it supposed to go up in the air?"

❦❦❦

Swing Thoughts

I ALWAYS EXPLAIN to my students about something called swing thoughts. For example, learning how to use them, how to find ones that work, and how to limit them. After the class where I explained this, a student came up to me and said, "Now what are those things called, are they range thoughts?"

❦❦❦

Hokey Pokey

"WHAT IF THE hokey pokey is all there is?"

I saw this bumper sticker on a car once and got a big kick out of it because I always tell my students to "do the hokey pokey" to loosen up. I tell them this jokingly, but sometimes they do dance around a little bit, which relaxes them.

But, really, what *if* the hokey pokey is all there is?

❧❧❧

Helicopters and Umbrellas

ONE WOMAN TOLD the story of hitting balls on the driving range. It was raining and she lost her club. It flew out of her hands over the range, helicoptering as it went. Each person on the range looked up as the club flew over their heads. It landed at the far end of the range.

The next day after this scary and funny episode, where luckily no one was injured, the woman bought what she told me was an umbrella.

I said, "An umbrella?"

"Yes," she said. "I got an umbrella 'policy,' not a real umbrella. I thought I better have one if I ended up knocking out any golfers when my club slips out of my hands again."

✿❧❧✿

Unabomber

A FEW YEARS back I organized a group of Californians to come to Montana for a golf and fly fishing outing. I made all the plans and hoped to rent a van to take them to the course and the fishing streams. I made a call to the car rental agency and the woman said, "You won't be able to find a van to rent at all anywhere around here. The FBI has rented all of them. They think they have tracked down the Unabomber."

She was right. The very next day, the story broke. Ted Kaczynski, the Unabomber, was arrested at his cabin near Lincoln, Montana, about an hour northeast of Missoula.

I believe I changed the dates for this trip to the following weekend, when there was van availability.

❦❦❦

Tee or Ti?

I TOOK A Spanish class and four of the people in the group were former golf students of mine. One of them said to me a week or so after we began her golf lessons, "No puedo jugar sin ti." I thought she meant she couldn't play without a "tee." I told her in Spanish that soon I would have her try swinging without using a golf tee. During the lessons I teed the ball up for her.

She replied, "No, yo no puedo jugar sin ti." Interpretation: "I can't play without you!"

Obviously, "ti" means "you" in Spanish. This is where the confusion and laughter came in!

❦❦❦

Smith Barney

I WAS TEACHING a group class on using the woods. The driving range was full of other golfers practicing. I purposely said a bit loudly, "Now I am going to tell you the secret of golf." I wanted all the golfers on the range to hear, because it was like that Smith Barney commercial where everyone stops what they are doing and cups their hand to their ear so they can hear the secret. As soon as I saw the other golfers who were not in the group perk up to listen, I whispered to each student in the group very quietly so it appeared that they were, indeed, receiving the secret to golf! What I whispered was, "There is no secret!" I wish I had a camera to record some of the looks I received. They were forlorn looks. No secret for them, at least not that day!

❧☙❧

Gophers

IT'S ALMOST A given that with golf comes humor. I have taught at various driving ranges in California. One particular range was going to be closing for development, and the owners were not spending money to grow grass. The range had a series of gopher holes throughout. On occasion, a gopher would pop his head up out of a hole somewhere on the range. It was somewhat reminiscent of that game called "Whack-A-Gopher."

I was conducting a women's golf school with my LPGA teaching associate, Barabara O'Brien. She and I ran a series of very successful golf schools. We had a number of private country club members from the San Francisco area who would drive an hour or so to attend.

I was helping one of the women with her full swing on the range. I think she was a member at the exclusive Olympic Club in San Francisco. She got into the address position and was all set to take a swing, when she let out a loud shriek. Unbeknownst to her, she had straddled a gopher hole. As she began her backswing, a gopher popped his head up right there between her legs. There she stood, frozen in fear, with the little smiling gopher amiably looking at her from between her feet.

Finally, he went back into his hole, but the poor woman was traumatized. It was so unexpected and almost like a scene out of Caddyshack!

Goats

AT THIS SAME driving range and at the same golf school, one of the attending students raised goats as a part-time hobby. One goat, in particular, was having some problems. She asked me if she could bring the goat to the range during the school. She said she would tie it to the fence off to the side. She said she needed to monitor it, and it couldn't be left alone all day. So she brought the goat and tied it up. It was a young goat. Ha, as if being an old goat would have made any difference! Well, what a mistake that was! Immediately, the young goat began braying loudly and jumping around. There was nowhere to take the goat, so all she could do was leave it tied to the fence. We spent the entire half-day school listening to that braying goat. It truly was a sad comedy. But what could we do? Who would've suspected that the young goat would act up like that all morning? This driving range was quickly becoming known for its gophers and goats, not its golf.

❧❦❧

Out of Step

I TAUGHT GOLF lessons in California for nine years. I gave half-hour lessons. I found that people were in a hurry and a lot of the golfers took a lesson over the lunch hour.

The guys usually came in, tucked their tie into their shirts, changed into their golf shoes, and were good to go. They got there a few minutes before the lesson, and departed right afterward.

I often wondered if they took much time with anything, and it seemed that their lives were a bit frenzied.

I had one student who was an interior designer. She came regularly once a week. She, too, would arrive and change out of her high heels to her tennis shoes and be good to go for the lesson. This time, I saw her coming to the lesson in her high heels and she was walking oddly. I looked at her and wondered if she had noticed what I did. She acted like nothing was wrong, but she was walking off balance and out of step.

I said to her, "Betty, did you know you have on two high heels, but they are not a match—one heel is much, much shorter than the other?"

She looked at me and exclaimed, "Oh my, no wonder my day has been off a bit!"

Title IX

I GREW UP when sports were not encouraged for girls. We were on our own, and cheerleading was about the only choice. It was very frustrating, and Title IX legislation did not come about until I graduated from college in 1974.

Recently, I had my teeth cleaned. The dental hygienist was in her early thirties and an avid biker, hiker and sports enthusiast. We were having a conversation about my golf business and how I created it.

She asked me, "Well, you played golf in college then, I would imagine."

I replied, "No, I was pre-Title IX."

She looked at me and said, "Oh, you mean that clothing company...I really like their clothing."

Perplexed, I looked back at her. She noticed my perplexed look, and exclaimed, "Oh no, you mean that sports drink?"

I said no and looked at her even a bit more perplexed.

She said, "Oh...oh, I know what you mean, you mean the Title-ist golf ball?"

Oh my!

"No." I replied, realizing that she did not know what I was talking about when I mentioned Title IX.

So, I explained it to her and she could not believe that there was legislation like this and that she, being a female athlete, knew nothing about it.

I found this little incident astonishing!

❧❦❦❧

Grandmother's Clubs

I HAD AN older woman come in for lessons who had been a softball player. She had her great-grandmother's (age 86) clubs and her great-grandmother's bag as well. For some reason, I kept glancing at the bag thinking her great-grandmother was standing there with she and I for the lesson.

Her husband purchased an hour lesson for her. He also put together a set of clubs for her from the sets of both of her grandmothers. So, she had three sets of old clubs.

This made quite a motley collection of clubs. All in all, there were around 50 clubs and three bags.

I find with lessons a lot of times the student will bring in an old set of clubs that their mother, father, or grandparents used and the clubs are very sentimental to them.

I even have one student whose mother passed away and she plans to make a mobile out of them for her front yard. I thought this was a great idea. She could keep the clubs and display them, but not use them on the course where old clubs make the game that much more challenging. As if we need that!

❧❧❧

Olympic Golf

I HAVE HAD the excitement of watching two Olympic champions try their hand at golf. One was Pablo Morales, Olympic champion swimmer, and the other was Kristi Yamaguchi, Olympic champion figure skater.

They both hit golf balls at the driving ranges where I taught in the Bay Area of California.

Kristi just took up the sport for fun and came to the range to hit balls with her sister. Pablo came to the range to practice and attempt to excel. He was a regular there who hit ball after ball. I am not sure what type of golfer he became, but he sure had long arms and big hands, all the better to swim the butterfly with and win all those medals.

As I thought about these athletes and saw their efforts, it became clear to me that to excel in golf, one has to be gifted as well as dedicated. Not everyone can do well in golf and turn professional. It takes a certain mindset. Through the years, I have come to realize it is rare to see many people who have the mindset and gifts to become accomplished golfers. Heck, Olympic athletes don't even have guarantees in golf. This is all the more reason for we mere mortals to keep on practicing!

❧❧❧❧

Korean Excursion

ONE OF THE more entertaining encounters I had with students revolves around a group of Korean women who were attending the university for a couple of weeks in the summer. They were all teachers. Of course, golf is very popular in Korea, especially for women. Teachers of any kind are highly revered there.

Their lessons with me lasted a couple of weeks. They kept asking, "Teacher, teacher, when can we hit the 'oods?"

They could not say the letter "w" so woods came out 'oods. It was quite cute.

This same group kept asking me to go on the golf course before they left. They wanted to take carts.

In Korea, golf is expensive, so they thought this was a great idea.

I got them lined up one evening to go on the course and I would guide.

When it was time to get to the first tee and hit the first shot after they were all loaded in the carts, they were hesitant to get out of the carts to hit.

I said, "Okay ladies, it's time to tee off!"

They all looked over at me and said gleefully, "No, no, teacher. We don't want to hit the ball, we just want to drive around golf course in cart."

So, that's what we proceeded to do. We drove around in the carts for an hour and they were happy as peas in a pod.

I tell you, that was the easiest money I've made in my career. All we did was drive around in golf carts. I pointed out golf course features, obstacles and the general layout of the course, but their focus was on driving the golf carts. They were gleeful.

At the end of the evening, they wanted to pose with the "teacher." I ended up signing lots of autographs as well. It was quite entertaining for all involved.

❧❧

Slices or Slants?

JUNIOR GOLFERS ALWAYS come up with the unexpected.

During my junior clinics, I hold up a club and tell the kids the name of each part of the club. Sometimes I have them try to guess, just to see the word they come up with.

One day, I asked the kids to tell me what a ball that goes left-to-right is called. Of course the answer is a slice.

But this little boy raised his hand and said calmly, "A slant."

I find this common. The kids answer with a related word, sometimes the same number of letters, but it's usually not the correct word.

❧❧❧

Preschoolers

I ALSO TEACH a group of preschoolers. They are very cute.

At the end of one day's session, I asked each child to tell one thing they learned that day. We spent the day talking about etiquette and putting.

One little girl looked at me for the longest time and thought and thought. I could tell she was having a hard time thinking of something to say before she finally replied, "No pets."

She must have just come up with that as she thought about etiquette and the no running on the greens, no talking, etc. Not at any time in the class had I mentioned a thing about pets.

This provided me with insight into the workings of the preschoolers' brains.

❧❦❧

Cabinetmaker

I HAD ANOTHER new golfer, a former cabinetmaker. He had strong hands and I told him he had a firm grip, which he knew.

I was talking to him about relaxing his grip and relaxing in general, when he recounted this story to me.

He was playing with his brother-in-law. The brother-in-law was a decent golfer. One day, he hit his ball into a flock of geese that were wandering around on the fairway.

The geese didn't move at all when the ball landed amidst them. The brother-in-law said, "Watch this." Holding his club, he proceeded to walk right into the midst of the gathered geese. He addressed his ball and hit it quite nicely. Then, he walked out of the flock of geese as they squawked, flapped their wings and made a huge fuss.

He said, "See."

The cabinetmaker really liked this story and the relaxed demeanor that his brother-in-law showed. He learned that it was an inner calm that the golfer searches for through this incident.

He said, "It sure helps to stay relaxed, because if my brother-in-law had been all huffy, puffy, and tense, the geese never would have let him get away with that shot."

❧❧❧❧

Mental and Physical Presence

I HAVE A student who shows horses. She says she has a hard time presenting the horses to the judge. She said she aims for the right shoulder of the judge because this helps her present directly in front of the judge. She does not know why she is so off on this. She has the same trouble putting. So, I had her imagine that she was aiming for the right shoulder of the judge, rather than at the judge (the hole), and this seemed to work for her.

Voila! All the putts were now on line.

As a teaching professional I always seek to work with what the student brings to the table. If I can discover something in their background they can relate to, it's much easier for both of us.

This student also mentioned that if you want your horse to walk, not trot, you better *think* walk. A slight body movement from the rider can indicate this to the horse.

This is an example of how a performer (rider/golfer) needs to "be in their body." This rare combination of mental and physical presence contributes to excellence on the golf course.

❧❧❧

Natural Creativity

LET'S GO BACK to the preschoolers. Their creativity is very natural. On the putting green, they wanted to tee up the ball. They are not so much concerned about putting and its technique as they are about finding little bugs crawling on the green. They are not linear at all in their thinking. They are totally into the moment, and into creativity very naturally. Watching kids play golf is a good pastime for adults. It helps us remember to **play**!

❀❧❧❀

Heart Surgery

I WAS GIVING a lesson to a top heart surgeon. I was demonstrating and discussing specialty shots. When in trouble, getting out of trouble in one swing is the top priority. This is the first thought the golfer should have. Above all, the golfer should not complicate the situation by trying an impossible shot and end up in worse shape than when they started.

The surgeon answered, "Yes, just like surgery…stop the bleeding first, and then move on."

I replied, "Yup, you've got it."

❀❧❧❀

The Bottom of the Top

ONE TIME, THE student kept on topping the ball. He looked at me in desperation.

With a slight smile and no panic at all, I exclaimed, "Don't worry, we'll get to the bottom of the top soon."

This word play lightened him up. Soon, he was not topping, was swinging with ease and was much more relaxed and happy.

❧❧❧❧

Golf as Saving Grace

ONE OF MY students had a heart replacement valve put in. He was in the hospital for five months. He was so happy to be out of the hospital and thrilled to be taking golf lessons.

In fact, he had been on a respirator eight different times!

This is golf as a saving grace! Golf gets the person out and moving without regard to an outcome.

Golf is good for many things aside from the inherent challenge of the sport. Among these are: recovering from broken relationships, recovering from physical problems, recovery from losing a spouse, and a chance to be in nature and regain a social aspect to one's life.

Golf gets a person out-of-doors, moving, interacting, and challenging oneself. What other game can do this?

❦❦

Scalped

MY GOLF COURSE manager is a decent golfer and he helped me teach a group of Native American kids one season. The program was part of a special grant to introduce the kids to new activities.

At the end of the session, we took them onto the golf course. We split the groups, half going with me and half going with him.

Back at the clubhouse after the kids left for the day, my manager couldn't contain himself.

He explained to his kids how the greenskeeper moves the golf cups/holes around each morning. He and the kids were bending down, examining the spot where the last hole had been replaced. The replacement to this particular hole appeared to be a bit mowed over on the top and there was not much grass. The kids were looking at it and wondering why it was like that.

So, without thinking, the manager said, "It looks like this hole has been scalped."

The kids looked sharply up at him. He politely tried to manage his way out of the verbal faux pas. It was one of those times where there was nothing he could do. The kids ended up laughing about it anyway. They understood.

🐝🐞🐞🐝

Extend, Extend

THE BACKSWING IS one of the more challenging positions for a golfer to work on. The golfer can't see the backswing during the swing. The only way to really perfect it is to stop there and have a professional insure that the correct position is attained.

One of the key ingredients to an efficient backswing is extension of the left arm. Proper and full extension maintains the radius of the swing and insures consistent solid contact.

I taught many lessons at the same facility as my early mentor and teaching associate, Barbra O'Brien. I will never forget the time she was working with a very short person who had very short arms. Barbra had the student stopped in the backswing and Barbra was exclaiming, "Extend, extend!"

I remember looking over at them and Barbra was pulling as hard as she could on the poor student's arms—which were extended as far as they were going to go. The look of anguish in the student's eyes combined with Barbra's determination made for a comical scenario.

Barbra and I still chuckle about this incident. We knew that the student was trying to do her best and so was Barbra. However, I got to witness firsthand that individual limitations exist. Our job as instructors is to acknowledge the limitations and work *with* them so the student makes progress.

Remember to extend, but don't disconnect!

❧❧

Mark Spitz

MARK SPITZ, EIGHT-TIME Olympic golf medal swimming champion, was in Missoula, Montana to sign autographs as part of a promotion.

I made it a point to go to the signing. I got in line for his autograph. I took a golf ball for him to sign because I thought that would be cool.

When it was my turn, I gave him the ball to sign and he said, "My son is on the Hooters mini-tour. I love to play golf, but it is much harder than swimming."

Even Olympic champions are stymied by golf! This is a good thing to remember as we advance in learning this wonderful game.

I was very happy to obtain a nice Titleist golf ball signed by Mark as well as two signed pictures of him in his Olympic prime.

❧❧❧

Run Over by a Golf Cart

HERE'S A STORY for the ages.

I was an assistant professional at a resort course in Austin, Texas. One day after work, my friend Janice, the boat broker, joined me for golf. She was not a seasoned golfer with regard to etiquette, etc. In fact, she had an aversion to etiquette and would always do the opposite of what I told her on the golf course. We used to laugh about this. She considered herself unteachable in this regard. Since she was a self-made woman, she was going to do what she wanted to do. That, after all, was the motif that gave her success in business. There was nothing I could do to change her mindset. This was one stubborn woman.

We hit our shots off the first tee. Janice hit her ball to the right into a grove of trees and possibly out of bounds. I drove the cart up the hill towards the out of bounds. I turned it facing downhill and put the parking brake on.

I got out to search for her ball. Janice remained in the cart in the passenger seat looking for her ball from there.

I did not find her ball, so I returned to the cart and walked in front of it (a three-wheeler) and put my hand on the bar supporting the cart ceiling as I swung around towards the driver's side.

Unfortunately, at this moment, Janice put her foot on the accelerator and the cart lurched forward and knocked me down. It proceeded to run me over. Janice, realizing what was happening, frantically tried to apply the brake, which was inches from stabbing me in the chest. I was thrown under the cart and being drug downhill. The last thing Janice saw was my Titleist visor disappearing under the cart.

What could have been a tragedy turned into a comedy, and Janice finally stopped the cart with me underneath it. I managed to not get run over completely, but I did have scrapes and my shirt and shorts were ripped.

When Janice realized what she had done, she leapt out of the cart, ran 20 yards and squatted down and went to the bathroom. Evidently, she was in shock and not sure of what to do, but at the same time, laughing uncontrollably.

I told Janice we needed to get out of there. She had just run over the assistant professional at the golf course. Soon more people would be on the first tee. We got in the cart, in a daze, and played three more holes. We realized that I was in no shape to play nor was she. We retreated to the local resort bar. We ordered our favorite drinks and told our story to those who were asking why my clothes were ripped. I remained in shock. Janice and I still reminisce over this event, 22 years later. It had traces of both comedy and tragedy. Lucky for both of us, comedy was the victor.

❧❧

Gyro Versus Euro

I WAS PLANNING my first golf trip to Ireland a few years back. I would be going with an old college chum who had enlisted me to teach her golf in Ireland.

She recommended I go to the bank in Missoula, Montana, where I resided to obtain some euros in advance of the trip. That way, I would be set when I arrived in Ireland and could take the bus to the city center in Dublin.

I went to the bank. I told the bank teller I wanted some euros.

She looked at me somewhat perplexed and after a few seconds said, "That sandwich shop is in the mall."

Stunned, I realized that she thought I had asked for gyros, not euros. In fact, she had no idea what a euro was. Seriously. No idea.

I laughed and explained it all to her and she went and got her manager and lo and behold, no euros were sold at this bank.

❧❧

Club Length

ONE TIME I took out all the irons in a golf bag and explained to the student how the clubs changed in both loft and length.

"Oh," she exclaimed with a look of shock on her face "They're all getting longer."

❧❧

Fly Fishing and Golf

ONE GOLF SEASON, I worked as an assistant professional at a small resort course in Seeley Lake, Montana, not far from Missoula.

An old man occasionally came to the shop for a cup of coffee. I would always chat a bit with him, but I could tell he was not a golfer; he just came for the coffee.

One week I had my fliers at the pro shop advertising a golf/fly fishing seminar that I co-hosted with Maggie Merriman, renowned fly fishing instructor.

This fellow picked up the flier said, "I know of Maggie. She is an excellent instructor."

And with that, nothing more was said.

A few days later, I came to work and there were two small boxes at the counter, one with my name, and one with Maggie's.

I opened my box and inside were 12 hand-tied flies with a card attached saying these flies were hand-tied by George Croonenburgh.

As it turns out, this was the man who came in for coffee occasionally.

About a week or so later, I was picking up range baskets at the end of the evening shift. A big wildfire was burning up the side of the mountain not too far away. There were two people inside a car parked nearby, watching the fire.

I went over to the car and there sat George Croonenburgh and his wife.

I thanked him for the flies. Then, rather unceremoniously, he picked up a string that was sitting in the car and he began to weave intricate patterns with it, as a magician would.

"Yes." he said. "I grew up here in Seeley Lake. I was best friends and neighbors with Norman McClean and I was the technical advisor for *The River Runs Through It* movie."

He went on to say that he liked working with Brad Pitt, but the other actor who played Norman McClean was more difficult to work with.

George had a relaxed presence to him and smiled a lot.

After that, I occasionally saw George in the post office.

One day he stopped and told me his wife had died. He was sad. He also told me how he had been a doorman years ago when doormen existed. He got a wistful look in his eyes.

He was around 90 at the time.

I wrote him a letter saying I was sorry he lost his wife and I received a nice note back from him.

Not long after, maybe a year or so, I read in the paper that George Croonenburgh, renowned fly fishing expert and best friend to Norman McClean, had died.

I was so happy that I spoke to him and became his friend those days when he came to the golf shop for coffee.

❧❧❧

Love Versus Hate

AN OLD HIGH school friend of mine who does not play golf, but would like to, was having a conversation with me by phone. We hadn't talked in a long time. I was explaining to her about my career and about playing golf in general.

After hearing all about my golf escapades, her comment was, "In one hole, you can love or hate the game, can't you?"

How telling was that?

❧❧❧

The Cart Before the Horse

ONE STUDENT TOLD me, "I want to get good before I spend money to play."

❦❦❦

Distracted to No End

I HAVE SOME students who are a bit absent-minded, or might I say, not that aware of their body movements. One woman came for her lesson. She had a check to pay for the lesson and stuck it in her brassiere. She planned to give it to me after the lesson. As she was swinging away and hitting balls, the check kept coming out and she kept stuffing it back into her brassiere. Talk about a distraction for her.

She also kept fussing with her glasses. She had them jerry-rigged with rubber bands because they were falling apart. Finally, she took them off and then she couldn't see.

Finally, I drove her back to her car in the cart so she could get another pair of glasses she could wear for the lesson.

When she handed me the check for the lesson, we both laughed. The ink had smeared from all her exertion, and she ended up using her credit card to pay for the lesson.

Bear with Me

ONE OF MY students is a real estate broker and she always arrived at her lesson on time. One day, however, she never showed up for her lesson. She didn't call to say she was running late, either. I waited, and then called her number. I got her voicemail. Finally, I received a return call from her that evening.

She said, "Oh, I am so sorry, Ann. I missed my lesson. But I have a good reason. I was driving along the highway coming to the lesson and I hit a black bear! That's why I never made it to the lesson."

In Montana, many pedestrians seem to be bears.

Rosie the Riveter

ONE OF MY students tells me that she feels like a Princess with her 7-wood and like Rosie the Riveter with her driver and 5-wood!

❧❦❧

Toot, Toot

I WAS WORKING with one woman on her follow through and finish. We were emphasizing that she hold this position. I said, "Now, hold that pretty finish." She replied, "I will, but I'm also trying not to toot!" She had not had lessons in 45 years and was a critical care nurse.

❧❦❧

Orientation

WHEN SOME OF my students are just starting out with golf, they are thrilled to have me drive them around the clubhouse and the driving range. I point out the tee boxes, putting green, range, range ball machine or bin, tee signs, etc. I usually take them into the pro shop and pull out a set of clubs, woods and irons. I show that the irons change length by a half-inch and the loft changes by four degrees per club. Lots of times, they say that no one has told them any of this. They are amazed by how light the woods are and I usually let them hold the ultra light titanium driver. This takes away some of the anxiety involved with coming to a golf lesson.

❧❦❧

Rodeo Roper

I HAVE A fellow who ran the YMCA in town for a long time. He's very athletic. He's in his 70s and shoots in the low 80s. He has three metal plates in his neck and four screws in his shoulder from past injuries. His direction with his irons had been off for a long time and he attributed it to the plates and screws, but wasn't sure.

As we proceeded through the lesson, I discovered that he was a National Champion Rodeo Roper. When we talked about this, it helped him relate to a lighter grip and to not force the swing. I explained the sequence of the swing. He could relate, with my guidance, to the correlations between golf and roping.

By the time he was done with the lesson, he was smiling up a storm and no longer hitting behind the ball. Plus, his direction was back on target. Because I was able to draw upon his previous roping experience, he was able to progress instantaneously.

❧❦❧❦

Winter in the Tree

ONE SPRING, A student played golf with her daughter and boyfriend. They came upon a ball wedged up in a tree and the boyfriend said, "That's my ball from last year up in that tree. I hit it there then and we couldn't get it down and it's still there. I guess it stayed there all winter."

❧❦❧❦

Craigslist Driver

ONE STUDENT'S GOAL was merely to get out and play a round of golf with her friends. She thought the first thing to do was to get a driver, so she went on Craigslist and bought one and came to the lesson with just that single club.

❧❧❧

No Improvement

CUTE COMMENT:

"My husband started me playing eight years ago and really, I'm doing better at driving the cart than I am at golf."

❧❧❧

Check your Face and Head

WHEN I SAY, "check your face" or "check your head," I have to explain because I have received a couple of odd looks. It seems the people were wondering if they needed to check their real face and head on their bodies, not their golf clubs. Some people take things very literally and just haven't learned golf jargon yet. It takes time.

❧❧❧

Peeking

ONE OF MY favorite and often used drills is called the eyes closed drill. The student closes his eyes and swings. If he is ok with that, I add a ball. This helps him get out of the seeing/thinking mode and get into the body mode.

As always, I ask the student, "Did you keep your eyes closed on that last swing?"

And he replied, "Only one of them, I peeked."

❧❧❧

Worrisome Clubhouse Rules

CUTE COMMENT:

"I have a vague idea of how to hold a club, but more than that, I'm worried about the sign that says, "Wear a collared shirt."

❧❧

Never Embarrassed

CUTE COMMENT:

"I hope I can be like my mother-in-law. She played for years and never got the ball off the ground and was never embarrassed."

❧❧

Too Loose

I TOLD ONE student to loosen his grip. We were chipping. I came up to him, took a hold of the club, and he made a stroke as I guided. As we stroked through, he let go of the club completely and I finished the stroke for him. There he stood with no club. There I was in his follow through, holding his club!

❧❦❧

Shipping Magnate

ONE WINTER I taught indoor lessons at Canyon Ranch, a high-end resort spa in Tucson, Arizona. People could sign up for a lesson with me through the front desk. I would have no idea of who was coming for the lesson until I saw their name that day.

One student had a very Greek name, and looked somewhat like Aristotle Onassis. Of course, we had many international visitors at this resort, so I assumed he was from Greece.

As I began asking the introductory questions to what turned out to be a very beginner, I discovered he wanted to learn the game for business purposes. I then said, "Ok, great. What is it that you do for your business?"

He looked at me very seriously and replied, "I am a shipping magnate and I live in Greece."

I must say, this is the only time I'd given golf lessons to a shipping magnate. The lesson went well and he was a very good student. I could tell he wasn't used to taking instruction from a female though. I'm sure in the world of shipping magnates there are not a lot of women.

❈❈❈

Consistency

CUTE COMMENT:

"I'm not consistent. I'm not even consistently bad."

❈❈❈

Repent

CUTE COMMENT:

"I have impure swing thoughts."

❈❈❈

Oklahoma!

A WOMAN FROM Oklahoma took her first lesson. She was visiting her daughter. Her daughter was worried about her mother because her husband died the past year. The daughter thought it would be a good idea to sign her mother up for golf lessons with me. They would take the lessons together. They took one lesson and the daughter scheduled a golf game for that afternoon. The mother planned to ride along and watch, but not play. When they returned two days later for lesson number two, I saw a huge, black and blue bruise around the mother's eye.

"Well," she said, "I was hit by a ball. It flew and hit me right near my eye. I was lucky it wasn't worse."

I told her this was a very rare occurrence and she should not lose hope. She said she would keep on with the lessons. And she did. On top of it all, the incident gave her a great story to tell her pals back in Oklahoma about her first day of golf.

✿✿✿✿

Tempo Tantrum

A FRIEND AND I were out playing one day when he swung way too fast and really chunked the shot. He turned to me and said, " I think I just had a tempo tantrum!"

✿✿✿

The Beverage Cart

OVERHEARD DURING A group lesson:
"What's your favorite part of the game?"
"The beverage cart."

✿✿✿

Miller Barber

I RAN INTO Miller Barber one day on the driving range. He was practicing. He said Harvey Penick told him one thing during a lesson years ago. Penick said, "It looks like you can play this game, so don't change a thing."

As my chat with Miller was ending and I was walking away, he said quietly to himself, "Tempo, tempo, tempo."

When he taught golf in New York in 1963 he said he didn't try to change anything, he just *helped* the golfer.

I was lucky enough to play golf with Miller Barber in his seniors pro am in Missoula, Montana one year. At the last minute, I filled in for astronaut Gene Cernan, who couldn't make it up from Texas. Here I was replacing the man who walked on the moon. I hoped my amateur playing partners weren't going to be disappointed when they were expecting Gene and got me!

❧❧❧❧

Age

OVERHEARD ON THE driving range:
   My health's ok, I'm just old."

❧❧❧❧

Bag Tag

I ASKED ONE student what their goal in golf was and they replied:
   "To take my new bag tag off my bag."
   And lastly…

❧❧❧

Retirement Plan

I AM LUCKY enough to have a group of golfers take lessons from me every year as well as follow me to Arizona to take more lessons in the winter. We have a lot of fun. They call themselves The Boondogglers and golf and party together. They are all past 50 years old and they say to me,

"We can't remember from year to year what you tell us, Ann, so we have to keep taking lessons. Anyway, you're lucky, because we are your 401k retirement plan!"

❧❧❧

In Closing

So, THAT'S IT in a nutshell. There is lots more to tell and lots more to experience. I am still teaching up a storm. More than anything, I remain thankful. Golf has provided me with a career where I have been able to laugh, inspire, influence, teach, lead, entertain and educate. Every day on the range or the golf course still provides a magical setting for me.

What more could I ask for? See you on the links!

In Gratitude

THE WRITING OF *The Golf Letters* has truly been a memorable experience for me. Along the way, I've had lots of encouragement and support as I connected the dots for this book and stayed the course.

Without the enchanting game of golf, this book would not have been possible. I salute the sport that provided me with years of opportunity to both teach and learn its truths.

Above all, I would like to thank the thousands of golf students who took lessons from me. What a ride we've had, haven't we?

At various times in the last few years, a sprinkling of people have guided me along this writing path. Dan Morgan continued to motivate me early on and told me I had not only one book, but a series of books in me—this inspired me.

Old friends Janice Siebert and Shari Lemke always encouraged me.

All of my LPGA and PGA professional pals, who are truly my compatriots in golf and in life, deserve a great big clap on the back. I love you all!

My six siblings and my mother Joanne and her husband Jack often wondered what I was up to, and now they know. And, if my father were alive, he might finally be convinced that a law career wasn't for me. Bless his soul.

Thank you Gail Cross for your design and layout work and for being so easy to work with.

Thank you Marge Hulburt for your early editing and interest in my writing.

Thank you Steve Pressfield—your Foreword nearly knocked me out of my golf spikes!

Thank you Printer Bowler—your way with words and your light touch are blessings, indeed.

Thank you Mary Loughlin—you are a sister of delight and your ease and bottom line approach were just what I needed in the editing.

And, finally, in gratitude to my heritage as an Irish woman who truly has embraced a life of joys in teaching.

Nothing could be finer.

~ Annie Loughlin